I0163109

The Strange Gentlemen - A Comic Burletta In Two Acts by Charles Dickens

Charles Dickens (1812-1870) is regarded by many readers and literary critics to be THE major English novelist of the Victorian Age. He is remembered today as the author of a series of weighty novels which have been translated into many languages and promoted to the rank of World Classics. The latter include, but are not limited to, *The Adventures of Oliver Twist*, *A Tale of Two Cities*, *David Copperfield*, *A Christmas Carol*, *Hard Times*, *Great Expectations* and *The Old Curiosity Shop*.

His talents extended to many other forms including short stories, poetry, letters and his serial magazines. Of course being such a talent he also wrote plays. We are very pleased to present his first of four plays first performed at St. James's Theatre, September 29, 1836

Index Of Contents

CAST OF THE CHARACTERS

MR. OWEN OVERTON (Mayor of a small town on the road to Gretna, and useful at the St. James's Arms) (Played by MR. HOLLINGSWORTH).

JOHN JOHNSON (detained at the St. James's Arms) (Played by MR. SIDNEY).

THE STRANGE GENTLEMAN (just arrived at the St. James's Arms) (Played by MR. HARLEY).

CHARLES TOMKINS (incognito at the St. James's Arms) (Played by MR. FORESTER).

TOM SPARKS (a one-eyed 'Boots' at the St. James's Arms) (Played by MR. GARDNER).

JOHN }		(Played by Mr Williamson)
TOM }	Waiters At The St James's Arms	(Played by Mr May)
WILL }		(Played by Mr Coulson)

JULIA DOBBS (looking for a husband at St. James's Arms) (Played by MADAME SALA).

FANNY WILSON (with an appointment at the St. James's Arms) (Played by MISS SMITH).

MARY WILSON (her sister, awkwardly situated at the St. James's Arms) (Played by MISS JULIA SMITH)

MRS. NOAKES (the Landlady at the St. James's Arms) (Played by MRS. W. PENSON).

CHAMBERMAID (at the St. James's Arms) (Played by MISS STUART).

Miss Smith and Miss Julia Smith will sing the duet of 'I know a Bank,' in 'The Strange Gentleman.'

COSTUME

MR. OWEN OVERTON.—Black smalls, and high black boots. A blue body coat, rather long in the waist, with yellow buttons, buttoned close up to the chin. A white stock; ditto gloves. A broad-brimmed low-crowned white hat.

STRANGE GENTLEMAN.—A light blue plaid French-cut trousers and vest. A brown cloth frock coat, with full skirts, scarcely covering the hips. A light blue kerchief, and eccentric low-crowned broad-brimmed white hat. Boots.

JOHN JOHNSON.—White fashionable trousers, boots, light vest, frock coat, black hat, gloves, etc.

CHARLES TOMKINS.—Shepherd's plaid French-cut trousers; boots; mohair fashionable frock coat, buttoned up; black hat, gloves, etc.

TOM SPARKS.—Leather smalls; striped stockings, and lace-up half boots, red vest, and a Holland stable jacket; coloured kerchief, and red wig.

THE WAITERS.—All in black trousers, black stockings and shoes, white vests, striped jackets, and white kerchiefs.

MARY WILSON.—Fashionable walking dress, white silk stockings; shoes and gloves.

FANNY WILSON.—Precisely the same as Mary.

JULIA DOBBS.—A handsome white travelling dress, cashmere shawl, white silk stockings; shoes and gloves. A bonnet to correspond.

MRS. NOAKES.—A chintz gown, rather of a dark pattern, French apron, and handsome cap.

SCENE.—A SMALL TOWN, ON THE ROAD TO GRETNA.

TIME.—PART OF A DAY AND NIGHT.

Time in acting.—One hour and twenty minutes.

THE STRANGE GENTLEMAN

ACT I

SCENE I.—A Room at the St. James's Arms; Door in Centre, with a Bolt on it. A Table with Cover, and two Chairs, R. H.

Enter MRS. NOAKES, C. DOOR.

MRS. NOAKES. Bless us, what a coachful! Four inside—twelve out; and the guard blowing the key-bugle in the fore-boot, for fear the informers should see that they have got one over the number. Post-chaise and a gig besides.—We shall be filled to the very attics. Now, look alive, there—bustle about.

Enter FIRST WAITER, running, C. DOOR.

Now, John.

FIRST WAITER (coming down L. H.). Single lady, inside the stage, wants a private room, ma'am.

MRS. NOAKES (R. H.). Much luggage?

FIRST WAITER. Four trunks, two bonnet-boxes, six brown-paper parcels, and a basket.

MRS. NOAKES. Give her a private room, directly. No. 1, on the first floor.

FIRST WAITER. Yes, ma'am.

[Exit FIRST WAITER, running, C. DOOR.

Enter SECOND WAITER, running, C. DOOR.

Now, Tom.

SECOND WAITER (coming down R. H.). Two young ladies and one gentleman, in a post-chaise, want a private sitting room d'rectly, ma'am.

MRS. NOAKES. Brother and sisters, Tom?

SECOND WAITER. Ladies are something alike, ma'am. Gentleman like neither of 'em.

MRS. NOAKES. Husband and wife and wife's sister, perhaps. Eh, Tom?

SECOND WAITER. Can't be husband and wife, ma'am, because I saw the gentleman kiss one of the ladies.

MRS. NOAKES. Kissing one of the ladies! Put them in the small sitting-room behind the bar, Tom, that I may have an eye on them through the little window, and see that nothing improper goes forward.

SECOND WAITER. Yes, ma'am. (Going.)

MRS. NOAKES. And Tom! (Crossing to L. H.)

SECOND WAITER. (coming down R. H.). Yes, ma'am.

MRS. NOAKES. Tell Cook to put together all the bones and pieces that were left on the plates at the great dinner yesterday, and make some nice soup to feed the stage-coach passengers with.

SECOND WAITER. Very well, ma'am.

[Exit SECOND WAITER, C. DOOR.

Enter THIRD WAITER, running, C. DOOR.

Now, Will.

THIRD WAITER (coming down L. H.). A strange gentleman in a gig, ma'am, wants a private sitting-room.

MRS. NOAKES. Much luggage, Will?

THIRD WAITER. One portmanteau, and a great-coat.

MRS. NOAKES. Oh! nonsense!—Tell him to go into the commercial room.

THIRD WAITER. I told him so, ma'am, but the Strange Gentleman says he will have a private apartment, and that it's as much as his life is worth, to sit in a public room.

MRS. NOAKES. As much as his life is worth?

THIRD WAITER. Yes, ma'am.—Gentleman says he doesn't care if it's a dark closet; but a private room of some kind he must and will have.

MRS. NOAKES. Very odd.—Did you ever see him before, Will?

THIRD WAITER. No, ma'am; he's quite a stranger here.—He's a wonderful man to talk, ma'am—keeps on like a steam engine. Here he is, ma'am.

STRANGE GENTLEMAN (without). Now don't tell me, because that's all gammon and nonsense; and gammoned I never was, and never will be, by any waiter that ever drew the breath of life, or a cork.—And just have the goodness to leave my portmanteau alone, because I can carry it very well myself; and show me a private room without further delay; for a private room I must and will have.—Damme, do you think I'm going to be murdered!—

Enter the three Waiters, C. DOOR—they form down L. H., the STRANGE GENTLEMAN following, carrying his portmanteau and great-coat.

There—this room will do capitally well. Quite the thing,—just the fit.—How are you, ma'am? I suppose you are the landlady of this place? Just order those very attentive young fellows out, will you, and I'll order dinner.

MRS. NOAKES (to Waiters). You may leave the room.

STRANGE GENTLEMAN. Hear that?—You may leave the room. Make yourselves scarce. Evaporate—disappear—come.

[Exeunt Waiters, C. DOOR.

That's right. And now, madam, while we're talking over this important matter of dinner, I'll just secure us effectually against further intrusion. (Bolts the door.)

MRS. NOAKES. Lor, sir! Bolting the door, and me in the room!

STRANGE GENTLEMAN. Don't be afraid—I won't hurt you. I have no designs against you, my dear ma'am: but I must be private. (Sits on the portmanteau, R. H.)

MRS. NOAKES. Well, sir—I have no objection to break through our rules for once; but it is not our way, when we're full, to give private rooms to solitary gentlemen, who come in a gig, and bring only one portmanteau. You're quite a stranger here, sir. If I'm not mistaken, it's your first appearance in this house.

STRANGE GENTLEMAN. You're right, ma'am. It is my first, my very first—but not my last, I can tell you.

MRS. NOAKES. No?

STRANGE GENTLEMAN. No (looking round him). I like the look of this place. Snug and comfortable—neat and lively. You'll very often find me at the St. James's Arms, I can tell you, ma'am.

MRS. NOAKES (aside). A civil gentleman. Are you a stranger in this town, sir?

STRANGE GENTLEMAN. Stranger! Bless you, no. I have been here for many years past, in the season.

MRS. NOAKES. Indeed!

STRANGE GENTLEMAN. Oh, yes. Put up at the Royal Hotel regularly for a long time; but I was obliged to leave it at last.

MRS. NOAKES. I have heard a good many complaints of it.

STRANGE GENTLEMAN. O! terrible! such a noisy house.

MRS. NOAKES. Ah!

STRANGE GENTLEMAN. Shocking! Din, din, din—Drum, drum, drum, all night. Nothing but noise, glare, and nonsense. I bore it a long time for old acquaintance sake; but what do you think they did at last, ma'am?

MRS. NOAKES. I can't guess.

STRANGE GENTLEMAN. Turned the fine Old Assembly Room into a stable, and took to keeping horses. I tried that too, but I found I couldn't stand it; so I came away, ma'am, and—and—here I am. (Rises).

MRS. NOAKES. And I'll be bound to say, sir, that you will have no cause to complain of the exchange.

STRANGE GENTLEMAN. I'm sure not, ma'am; I know it—I feel it, already.

MRS. NOAKES. About dinner, sir; what would you like to take?

STRANGE GENTLEMAN. Let me see; will you be good enough to suggest something, ma'am?

MRS. NOAKES. Why, a broiled fowl and mushrooms is a very nice dish.

STRANGE GENTLEMAN. You are right, ma'am; a broiled fowl and mushrooms form a very delightful and harmless amusement, either for one or two persons. Broiled fowl and mushrooms let it be, ma'am.

MRS. NOAKES. In about an hour, I suppose, sir?

STRANGE GENTLEMAN. For the second time, ma'am, you have anticipated my feelings.

MRS. NOAKES. You'll want a bed to-night, I suppose, sir; perhaps you'd like to see it? Step this way, sir, and—(going L. H.).

STRANGE GENTLEMAN. No, no, never mind. (Aside.) This is a plot to get me out of the room. She's bribed by somebody who wants to identify me. I must be careful; I am exposed to nothing but artifice and stratagem. Never mind, ma'am, never mind.

MRS. NOAKES. If you'll give me your portmanteau, sir, the Boots will carry it into the next room for you.

STRANGE GENTLEMAN (aside.) Here's diabolical ingenuity; she thinks it's got the name upon it. (To her.) I'm very much obliged to the Boots for his disinterested attention, ma'am, but with your kind permission this portmanteau will remain just exactly where it is; consequently, ma'am, (with great warmth,) if the aforesaid Boots wishes to succeed in removing this portmanteau, he must previously remove me, ma'am, me; and it will take a pair of very stout Boots to do that, ma'am, I promise you.

MRS. NOAKES. Dear me, sir, you needn't fear for your portmanteau in this house; I dare say nobody wants it.

STRANGE GENTLEMAN. I hope not, ma'am, because in that case nobody will be disappointed. (Aside.) How she fixes her old eyes on me!

MRS. NOAKES (aside). I never saw such an extraordinary person in all my life. What can he be? (Looks at him very hard.)

[Exit MRS. NOAKES, C. DOOR.

STRANGE GENTLEMAN. She's gone at last! Now let me commune with my own dreadful thoughts, and reflect on the best means of escaping from my horrible position. (Takes a letter from his pocket.) Here's an illegal death-warrant; a pressing invitation to be slaughtered; a polite request just to step out and be killed, thrust into my hand by some disguised assassin in a dirty black calico jacket, the very instant I got out of the gig at the door. I know the hand; there's a ferocious recklessness in the cross to this 'T,' and a baleful malignity in the dot of that 'I,' which warns me that it comes from my desperate rival. (Opens it, and reads.) 'Mr. Horatio Tinkles'—that's him—'presents his compliments to his enemy'—that's me—'and requests the pleasure of his company to-morrow morning, under the clump of trees, on Corpse Common,'—Corpse Common!—'to which any of the town's people will direct him, and where he hopes to have the satisfaction of giving him his gruel.'—Giving him his gruel! Ironical cut-throat!—'His punctuality will be esteemed a personal favour, as it will save Mr. Tinkles the trouble and inconvenience of calling with a horsewhip in his pocket. Mr. Tinkles has ordered breakfast at the Royal for one. It is paid for. The individual who returns alive can eat it. Pistols—half-past five—precisely.'—Bloodthirsty miscreant! The individual who returns alive! I have seen him hit the painted man at the shooting-gallery regularly every time in his centre shirt plait, except when he varied the entertainments, by lodging the ball playfully in his left eye. Breakfast! I shall want nothing beyond the gruel. What's to be done? Escape! I can't escape; concealment's of no use, he knows I am here. He has dodged me all the way from London, and will dodge me all the way to the residence of Miss Emily Brown, whom my respected, but swine-headed parents have picked out for my future wife. A pretty figure I should cut before the old people, whom I have never beheld more than once in my life, and Miss Emily Brown, whom I have never seen at all, if I went down there, pursued by this Salamander, who, I suppose, is her accepted lover! What is to be done? I can't go back again; father would be furious. What can be done? nothing! (Sinks into a chair.) I must undergo this fiery ordeal, and submit to be packed up, and carried back to my weeping parents, like an unfortunate buck, with a flat piece of lead in my head, and a brief epitaph on my breast, 'Killed on Wednesday morning.' No, I won't (starting up, and walking about). I won't submit to it; I'll accept the challenge, but first I'll write an anonymous letter to the local authorities, giving them information of this intended duel, and desiring them to place me under immediate restraint. That's feasible; on further consideration, it's capital. My character will be saved—I shall be bound over—he'll be bound over—I shall resume my journey—reach the house—marry the girl—pocket the fortune, and laugh at him. No time to be lost; it shall be done forthwith. (Goes to the table and writes.) There; the challenge accepted, with a bold defiance, that'll look very brave when it comes to be printed. Now for the other. (Writes.) 'To the Mayor—Sir—A strange Gentleman at the St. James's Arms, whose name is unknown to the writer of this communication, is bent upon committing a rash and sanguinary act, at an early hour tomorrow morning. As you value human life, secure the amiable youth, without delay. Think, I implore you, sir, think what would be the feelings of those to whom he is nearest and dearest, if any mischance befall the interesting young man. Do not neglect this solemn warning; the number of his room is seventeen.' There—(folding it up). Now if I can find any one who will deliver it secretly.—

TOM SPARKS, with a pair of boots in his hand, peeps in at the C. D.

TOM. Are these here your'n?

STRANGE GENTLEMAN. No.

TOM. Oh! (going back).

STRANGE GENTLEMAN. Hallo! stop, are you the Boots?

TOM (still at the door). I'm the head o' that branch o' the establishment. There's another man under me, as brushes the dirt off, and puts the blacking on. The fancy work's my department; I do the polishing, nothing else.

STRANGE GENTLEMAN. You are the upper Boots, then?

TOM. Yes, I'm the reg'lar; t'other one's only the deputy; top boots and half boots, I calls us.

STRANGE GENTLEMAN. You're a sharp fellow.

TOM. Ah! I'd better cut then (going).

STRANGE GENTLEMAN. Don't hurry, Boots—don't hurry; I want you. (Rises, and comes forward, R.H.)

TOM (coming forward, L. H.). Well!

STRANGE GENTLEMAN. Can—can—you be secret, Boots?

TOM. That depends entirely on accompanying circumstances;—see the point?

STRANGE GENTLEMAN. I think I comprehend your meaning, Boots, You insinuate that you could be secret (putting his hand in his pocket) if you had—five shillings for instance—isn't that it, Boots?

TOM. That's the line o' argument I should take up; but that an't exactly my meaning.

STRANGE GENTLEMAN. No!

TOM. No. A secret's a thing as is always a rising to one's lips. It requires an astonishing weight to keep one on 'em down.

STRANGE GENTLEMAN. Ah!

TOM. Yes; I don't think I could keep one snug—reg'lar snug, you know—

STRANGE GENTLEMAN. Yes, regularly snug, of course.

TOM. —If it had a less weight a-top on it, than ten shillins.

STRANGE GENTLEMAN. You don't think three half-crowns would do it?

TOM. It might, I won't say it wouldn't, but I couldn't warrant it.

STRANGE GENTLEMAN. You could the other!

TOM. Yes.

STRANGE GENTLEMAN. Then there it is. (Gives him four half-crowns.) You see these letters?

TOM. Yes, I can manage that without my spectacles.

STRANGE GENTLEMAN. Well; that's to be left at the Royal Hotel. This, this, is an anonymous one; and I want it to be delivered at the Mayor's house, without his knowing from whom it came, or seeing who delivered it.

TOM (taking the letters). I say—you're a rum 'un, you are.

STRANGE GENTLEMAN. Think so! Ha, ha! so are you.

TOM. Ay, but you're a rummer one than me.

STRANGE GENTLEMAN. No, no, that's your modesty.

TOM. No it ain't. I say, how well you did them last hay-stacks. How do you contrive that ere now, if it's a fair question. Is it done with a pipe, or do you use them Lucifer boxes?

STRANGE GENTLEMAN. Pipe—Lucifer boxes—hay-stacks! Why, what do you mean?

TOM (looking cautiously round). I know your name, old 'un.

STRANGE GENTLEMAN. You know my name! (Aside.) Now how the devil has he got hold of that, I wonder!

TOM. Yes, I know it. It begins with a 'S.'

STRANGE GENTLEMAN. Begins with an S!

TOM. And ends with a 'G,' (winking). We've all heard talk of Swing down here.

STRANGE GENTLEMAN. Heard talk of Swing! Here's a situation! Damme, d'ye think I'm a walking carbois of vitriol, and burn everything I touch?—Will you go upon the errand you're paid for?

TOM. Oh, I'm going—I'm going. It's nothing to me, you know; I don't care. I'll only just give these boots to the deputy, to take them to whoever they belong to, and then I'll pitch this here letter in at the Mayor's office-window, in no time.

STRANGE GENTLEMAN. Will you be off?

TOM. Oh, I'm going, I'm going. Close, you knows, close!

[Exit TOM, C. DOOR.

STRANGE GENTLEMAN. In five minutes more the letter will be delivered; in another half hour, if the Mayor does his duty, I shall be in custody, and secure from the vengeance of this infuriated monster. I wonder whether they'll take me away? Egad! I may as well be provided with a clean shirt and a nightcap in case. Let's see, she said the next room was my bedroom, and as I have accepted the challenge, I may venture so far now. (Shouldering the portmanteau.) What a capital notion it is; there'll be all the correspondence in large letters, in the county paper, and my name figuring away in roman capitals, with a long story, how I was such a desperate dragon, and so bent upon fighting, that it took four constables to carry me to the Mayor, and one boy to carry my hat. It's a capital plan—must be done—the only way I have of escaping unpursued from this place, unless I could put myself in the General Post, and direct myself to a friend in town. And then it's a chance whether they'd take me in, being so much over weight.

[Exit STRANGE GENTLEMAN, with portmanteau, L. H.

MRS. NOAKES, peeping in C. DOOR, then entering.

MRS. NOAKES. This is the room, ladies, but the gentleman has stepped out somewhere, he won't be long, I dare say. Pray come in, Miss.

Enter MARY and FANNY WILSON, C. DOOR.

MARY (C.). This is the Strange Gentleman's apartment, is it?

MRS. NOAKES (R.). Yes, Miss; shall I see if I can find him, ladies, and tell him you are here?

MARY. No; we should prefer waiting till he returns, if you please.

MRS. NOAKES. Very well, ma'am. He'll be back directly, I dare say; for it's very near his dinner time.

[Exit MRS. NOAKES, C. DOOR.

MARY. Come, Fanny, dear; don't give way to these feelings of depression. Take pattern by me—I feel the absurdity of our situation acutely; but you see that I keep up, nevertheless.

FANNY. It is easy for you to do so. Your situation is neither so embarrassing, nor so painful a one as mine.

MARY. Well, my dear, it may not be, certainly; but the circumstances which render it less so are, I own, somewhat incomprehensible to me. My harebrained, mad-cap swain, John Johnson, implores me to leave my guardian's house, and accompany him on an expedition to Gretna Green. I with immense reluctance, and after considerable pressing—

FANNY. Yield a very willing consent.

MARY. Well, we won't quarrel about terms; at all events I do consent. He bears me off, and when we get exactly half-way, discovers that his money is all gone, and that we must stop at this Inn, until he can procure a remittance from London, by post. I think, my dear, you'll own that this is rather an embarrassing position.

FANNY. Compare it with mine. Taking advantage of your flight, I send express to my admirer, Charles Tomkins, to say that I have accompanied you; first, because I should have been miserable if left behind with a peevish old man alone; secondly, because I thought it proper that your sister should accompany you—

MARY. And, thirdly, because you knew that he would immediately comply with this indirect assent to his entreaties of three months' duration, and follow you without delay, on the same errand. Eh, my dear?

FANNY. It by no means follows that such was my intention, or that I knew he would pursue such a course, but supposing he has done so; supposing this Strange Gentleman should be himself—

MARY. Supposing!—Why, you know it is. You told him not to disclose his name, on any account; and the Strange Gentleman is not a very common travelling name, I should imagine; besides the hasty note, in which he said he should join you here.

FANNY. Well, granted that it is he. In what a situation am I placed. You tell me, for the first time, that my violent intended must on no account be beheld by your violent intended, just now, because of some old quarrel between them, of long standing, which has never been adjusted to this day. What an appearance this will have! How am I to explain it, or relate your present situation? I should sink into the earth with shame and confusion.

MARY. Leave it to me. It arises from my heedlessness. I will take it all upon myself and see him alone. But tell me, my dear—as you got up this love affair with so much secrecy and expedition during the four months you spent at Aunt Martha's, I have never yet seen Mr. Tomkins, you know. Is he so very handsome?

FANNY. See him, and judge for yourself.

MARY. Well, I will; and you may retire, till I have paved the way for your appearance. But just assist me first, dear, in making a little noise to attract his attention, if he really be in the next room, or I may wait here all day.

DUET—At end of which exit FANNY, C. DOOR. MARY retires up R. H.

Enter STRANGE GENTLEMAN, L. H.

STRANGE GENTLEMAN. There; now with a clean shirt in one pocket and a night-cap in the other, I'm ready to be carried magnanimously to my dungeon in the cause of love.

MARY (aside). He says, he's ready to be carried magnanimously to a dungeon in the cause of love. I thought it was Mr. Tomkins! Hem! (Coming down L. H.)

STRANGE GENTLEMAN (seeing her). Hallo! Who's this! Not a disguised peace officer in petticoats. Beg your pardon, ma'am. (Advancing towards her.) What—did—you—

MARY. Oh, Sir; I feel the delicacy of my situation.

STRANGE GENTLEMAN (aside). Feels the delicacy of her situation; Lord bless us, what's the matter! Permit me to offer you a seat, ma'am, if you're in a delicate situation. (He places chairs; they sit.)

MARY. You are very good, Sir. You are surprised to see me here, Sir?

STRANGE GENTLEMAN. No, no, at least not very; rather, perhaps—rather. (Aside.) Never was more astonished in all my life!

MARY (aside). His politeness, and the extraordinary tale I have to tell him, overpower me. I must summon up courage. Hem!

STRANGE GENTLEMAN. Hem!

MARY. Sir!

STRANGE GENTLEMAN. Ma'am!

MARY. You have arrived at this house in pursuit of a young lady, if I mistake not?

STRANGE GENTLEMAN. You are quite right, ma'am. (Aside.) Mysterious female!

MARY. If you are the gentleman I'm in search of, you wrote a hasty note a short time since, stating that you would be found here this afternoon.

STRANGE GENTLEMAN (drawing back his chair). I—I—wrote a note, ma'am!

MARY. You need keep nothing secret from me, Sir. I know all.

STRANGE GENTLEMAN (aside). That villain, Boots, has betrayed me! Know all, ma'am?

MARY. Everything.

STRANGE GENTLEMAN (aside). It must be so. She's a constable's wife.

MARY. You are the writer of that letter, Sir? I think I am not mistaken.

STRANGE GENTLEMAN. You are not, ma'am; I confess I did write it. What was I to do, ma'am? Consider the situation in which I was placed.

MARY. In your situation, you had, as it appears to me, only one course to pursue.

STRANGE GENTLEMAN. You mean the course I adopted?

MARY. Undoubtedly.

STRANGE GENTLEMAN. I am very happy to hear you say so, though of course I should like it to be kept a secret.

MARY. Oh, of course.

STRANGE GENTLEMAN (drawing his chair close to her, and speaking very softly). Will you allow me to ask you, whether the constables are downstairs?

MARY (surprised). The constables!

STRANGE GENTLEMAN. Because if I am to be apprehended, I should like to have it over. I am quite ready, if it must be done.

MARY. No legal interference has been attempted. There is nothing to prevent your continuing your journey to-night.

STRANGE GENTLEMAN. But will not the other party follow?

MARY (looking down). The other party, I am compelled to inform you, is detained here by—by want of funds.

STRANGE GENTLEMAN (starting up). Detained here by want of funds! Hurrah! Hurrah! I have caged him at last. I'm revenged for all his blustering and bullying. This is a glorious triumph, ha, ha, ha! I have nailed him—nailed him to the spot!

MARY (rising indignantly). This exulting over a fallen foe, Sir, is mean and pitiful. In my presence, too, it is an additional insult.

STRANGE GENTLEMAN. Insult! I wouldn't insult you for the world, after the joyful intelligence you have brought me—I could hug you in my arms!—One kiss, my little constable's deputy. (Seizing her).

MARY (struggling with him). Help! help!

Enter JOHN JOHNSON, C. DOOR.

JOHN. What the devil do I see! (Seizes STRANGE GENTLEMAN by the collar.)

MARY (L. H.). John, and Mr. Tomkins, met together! They'll kill each other. Here, help! help!

[Exit MARY, running, C. DOOR.

JOHN (shaking him). What do you mean by that, scoundrel?

STRANGE GENTLEMAN. Come, none of your nonsense—there's no harm done.

JOHN. No harm done. How dare you offer to salute that lady?

STRANGE GENTLEMAN. What did you send her here for?

JOHN. I send her here!

STRANGE GENTLEMAN. Yes, you; you gave her instructions, I suppose. (Aside.) Her husband, the constable, evidently.

JOHN. That lady, Sir, is attached to me.

STRANGE GENTLEMAN. Well, I know she is; and a very useful little person she must be, to be attached to anybody, it's a pity she can't be legally sworn in.

JOHN. Legally sworn in! Sir, that is an insolent reflection upon the temporary embarrassment which prevents our taking the marriage vows. How dare you to insinuate—

STRANGE GENTLEMAN. Pooh! pooh!—don't talk about daring to insinuate; it doesn't become a man in your station of life—

JOHN. My station of life!

STRANGE GENTLEMAN. But as you have managed this matter very quietly, and say you're in temporary embarrassment—here—here's five shillings for you. (Offers it.)

JOHN. Five shillings! (Raises his cane.)

STRANGE GENTLEMAN (flourishing a chair). Keep off, sir!

Enter MARY, TOM SPARKS, and two Waiters.

MARY. Separate them, or there'll be murder! (TOM clasps STRANGE GENTLEMAN round the waist— the Waiters seize JOHN JOHNSON).

TOM. Come, none o' that 'ere, Mr. S. We don't let private rooms for such games as these.—If you want to try it on wery partickler, we don't mind making a ring for you in the yard, but you mustn't do it here.

JOHN. Let me get at him. Let me go; waiters—Mary, don't hold me. I insist on your letting me go.

STRANGE GENTLEMAN. Hold him fast.—Call yourself a peace officer, you prize-fighter!

JOHN (struggling). Let me go, I say!

STRANGE GENTLEMAN. Hold him fast! Hold him fast!

[TOM takes STRANGE GENTLEMAN off, R. H.

Waiters take JOHN off, L. H. MARY following.

SCENE II.—Another Room in the Inn.

Enter JULIA DOBBS and OVERTON, L. H.

JULIA. You seem surprised, Overton.

OVERTON. Surprised, Miss Dobbs! Well I may be, when, after seeing nothing of you for three years and more, you come down here without any previous notice, for the express purpose of running away—positively running away, with a young man. I am astonished, Miss Dobbs!

JULIA. You would have had better reason to be astonished if I had come down here with any notion of positively running away with an old one, Overton.

OVERTON. Old or young, it would matter little to me, if you had not conceived the preposterous idea of entangling me—me, an attorney, and mayor of the town, in so ridiculous a scheme.—Miss Dobbs, I can't do it.—I really cannot consent to mix myself up with such an affair.

JULIA. Very well, Overton, very well. You recollect that in the lifetime of that poor old dear, Mr. Woolley, who—

OVERTON.—Who would have married you, if he hadn't died; and who, as it was, left you his property, free from all incumbrances, the incumbrance of himself, as a husband, not being among the least.

JULIA. Well, you may recollect, that in the poor old dear's lifetime, sundry advances of money were made to you, at my persuasion, which still remain unpaid. Oblige me by forwarding them to my agent in the course of the week, and I free you from any interference in this little matter. (Crosses to L. H. and is going.)

OVERTON. Stay, Miss Dobbs, stay. As you say, we are old acquaintances, and there certainly were some small sums of money, which—which—

JULIA. Which certainly are still outstanding.

OVERTON. Just so, just so; and which, perhaps, you would be likely to forget, if you had a husband—eh, Miss Dobbs, eh?

JULIA. I have little doubt that I should. If I gained one through your assistance, indeed—I can safely say I should forget all about them.

OVERTON. My dear Miss Dobbs, we perfectly understand each other.—Pray proceed.

JULIA. Well—dear Lord Peter—

OVERTON. That's the young man you're going to run away with, I presume?

JULIA. That's the young nobleman who's going to run away with me, Mr. Overton.

OVERTON. Yes, just so.—I beg your pardon—pray go on.

JULIA. Dear Lord Peter is young and wild, and the fact is, his friends do not consider him very sagacious or strong-minded. To prevent their interference, our marriage is to be a secret one. In fact, he is stopping now at a friend's hunting seat in the neighbourhood; he is to join me here; and we are to be married at Gretna.

OVERTON. Just so.—A matter, as it seems to me, which you can conclude without any interference.

JULIA. Wait an instant. To avoid suspicion, and prevent our being recognised and followed, I settled with him that you should give out in this house that he was a lunatic, and that I—his aunt—was going to convey him in a chaise, to-night, to a private asylum at Berwick. I have ordered the chaise at half-past one in the morning. You can see him, and make our final arrangements. It will avert all suspicion, if I have no communication with him, till we start. You can say to the people of the house that the sight of me makes him furious.

OVERTON. Where shall I find him?—Is he here?

JULIA. You know best.

OVERTON. I!

JULIA. I desired him, immediately on his arrival, to write you some mysterious nonsense, acquainting you with the number of his room.

OVERTON (producing a letter). Dear me, he has arrived, Miss Dobbs.

JULIA. No!

OVERTON. Yes—see here—a most mysterious and extraordinary composition, which was thrown in at my office window this morning, and which I could make neither head nor tail of. Is that his handwriting? (Giving her the letter.)

JULIA (taking letter). I never saw it more than once, but I know he writes very large and straggling.— (Looks at letter.) Ha, ha, ha! This is capital, isn't it?

OVERTON. Excellent!—Ha, ha, ha!—So mysterious!

JULIA. Ha, ha, ha!—So very good—'Rash act.'

OVERTON. Yes. Ha, ha!

JULIA. 'Interesting young man.'

OVERTON. Yes.—Very good.

JULIA. 'Amiable youth!'

OVERTON. Capital!

JULIA. 'Solemn warning!'

OVERTON. Yes.—That's the best of all. (They both laugh.)

JULIA. Number seventeen, he says. See him at once, that's a good creature. (Returning the letter.)

OVERTON (taking letter). I will. (He crosses to L. H. and rings a bell.)

Enter WAITER, L. H.

Who is there in number seventeen, waiter?

WAITER. Number seventeen, sir?—Oh!—the strange gentleman, sir.

OVERTON. Show me the room.

[Exit WAITER, L. H.

(Looking at JULIA, and pointing to the letter.) 'The Strange Gentleman.'—Ha, ha, ha! Very good—very good indeed.—Excellent notion! (They both laugh.)

[Exeunt severally.

SCENE III.—Same as the first.—A small table, with wine, dessert, and lights on it, R. H. of C. DOOR; two chairs.

STRANGE GENTLEMAN discovered seated at table.

STRANGE GENTLEMAN. 'The other party is detained here, by want of funds.' Ha, ha, ha! I can finish my wine at my leisure, order my gig when I please, and drive on to Brown's in perfect security. I'll drink the other party's good health, and long may he be detained here. (Fills a glass.) Ha, ha, ha! The other party; and long may he—(A knock at C. DOOR.) Hallo! I hope this isn't the other party. Talk of the—(A knock at C. DOOR.) Well—(setting down his glass)—this is the most extraordinary private room that was ever invented. I am continually disturbed by unaccountable knockings. (A gentle tap at C. DOOR.) There's another; that was a gentle rap—a persuasive tap—like a friend's fore-finger on one's coat-sleeve. It can't be Tinkles with the gruel.—Come in.

OVERTON peeping in at C. DOOR.

OVERTON. Are you alone, my Lord?

STRANGE GENTLEMAN (amazed). Eh!

OVERTON. Are you alone, my Lord?

STRANGE GENTLEMAN. My Lord!

OVERTON (stepping in, and closing the door). You are right, sir, we cannot be too cautious, for we do not know who may be within hearing. You are very right, sir.

STRANGE GENTLEMAN (rising from table, and coming forward, R. H.). It strikes me, sir, that you are very wrong.

OVERTON. Very good, very good; I like this caution; it shows me you are wide awake.

STRANGE GENTLEMAN. Wide awake!—damme, I begin to think I am fast asleep, and have been for the last two hours.

OVERTON (whispering). I—am—the mayor.

STRANGE GENTLEMAN (in the same tone). Oh!

OVERTON. This is your letter? (Shows it; STRANGE GENTLEMAN nods assent solemnly.) It will be necessary for you to leave here to-night, at half-past one o'clock, in a postchaise and four; and the higher you bribe the postboys to drive at their utmost speed, the better.

STRANGE GENTLEMAN. You don't say so?

OVERTON. I do indeed. You are not safe from pursuit here.

STRANGE GENTLEMAN. Bless my soul, can such dreadful things happen in a civilised community, Mr. Mayor?

OVERTON. It certainly does at first sight appear rather a hard case that people cannot marry whom they please, without being hunted down in this way.

STRANGE GENTLEMAN. To be sure. To be hunted down, and killed, as if one was game, you know.

OVERTON. Certainly, and you an't game, you know.

STRANGE GENTLEMAN. Of course not. But can't you prevent it? can't you save me by the interposition of your power?

OVERTON. My power can do nothing in such a case.

STRANGE GENTLEMAN. Can't it, though?

OVERTON. Nothing whatever.

STRANGE GENTLEMAN. I never heard of such dreadful revenge, never! Mr. Mayor, I am a victim, I am the unhappy victim of parental obstinacy.

OVERTON. Oh, no; don't say that. You may escape yet.

STRANGE GENTLEMAN (grasping his hand). Do you think I may? Do you think I may, Mr. Mayor?

OVERTON. Certainly! certainly! I have little doubt of it, if you manage properly.

STRANGE GENTLEMAN. I thought I was managing properly. I understood the other party was detained here, by want of funds.

OVERTON. Want of funds!—There's no want of funds in that quarter, I can tell you.

STRANGE GENTLEMAN. An't there, though?

OVERTON. Bless you, no. Three thousand a year!—But who told you there was a want of funds?

STRANGE GENTLEMAN. Why, she did.

OVERTON. She! you have seen her then? She told me you had not.

STRANGE GENTLEMAN. Nonsense; don't believe her. She was in this very room half an hour ago.

OVERTON. Then I must have misunderstood her, and you must have misunderstood her too.—But to return to business. Don't you think it would keep up appearances if I had you put under some restraint.

STRANGE GENTLEMAN. I think it would. I am very much obliged to you. (Aside.) This regard for my character in an utter stranger, and in a Mayor too, is quite affecting.

OVERTON. I'll send somebody up, to mount guard over you.

STRANGE GENTLEMAN. Thank 'ee, my dear friend, thank 'ee.

OVERTON. And if you make a little resistance, when we take you upstairs to your bedroom, or away in the chaise, it will be keeping up the character, you know.

STRANGE GENTLEMAN. To be sure.—So it will.—I'll do it.

OVERTON. Very well, then. I shall see your Lordship again by and by.—For the present, my Lord, good evening. (Going.)

STRANGE GENTLEMAN. Lord!—Lordship!—Mr. Mayor!

OVERTON. Eh?—Oh!—I see. (Comes forward.) Practising the lunatic, my Lord. Ah, very good—very vacant look indeed.—Admirable, my Lord, admirable!—I say, my Lord—(pointing to letter)—'Amiable youth!'—'Interesting young man.'—'Strange Gentleman.'—Eh? Ha, ha, ha! Knowing trick indeed, my Lord, very!

[Exit OVERTON, C. D.

STRANGE GENTLEMAN. That mayor is either in the very last stage of mystified intoxication, or in the most hopeless state of incurable insanity.—I have no doubt of it. A little touched here (tapping his forehead). Never mind, he is sufficiently sane to understand my business at all events. (Goes to table and takes a glass.) Poor fellow!—I'll drink his health, and speedy recovery. (A knock at C. DOOR.) It is a most extraordinary thing, now, that every time I propose a toast to myself, some confounded fellow raps at that door, as if he were receiving it with the utmost enthusiasm. Private room!—I might as well be sitting behind the little shutter of a Two-penny Post Office, where all the letters put in were to be post-paid. (A knock at C. DOOR.) Perhaps it's the guard! I shall feel a great deal safer if it is. Come in. (He has brought a chair forward, and sits L. H.)

Enter TOM SPARKS, C. DOOR, very slowly, with an enormous stick. He closes the door, and, after looking at the STRANGE GENTLEMAN very steadily, brings a chair down L. H., and sits opposite him.

STRANGE GENTLEMAN. Are you sent by the mayor of this place, to mount guard over me?

TOM. Yes, yes.—It's all right.

STRANGE GENTLEMAN (aside). It's all right—I'm safe. (To TOM, with affected indignation.) Now mind, I have been insulted by receiving this challenge, and I want to fight the man who gave it me. I protest against being kept here. I denounce this treatment as an outrage.

TOM. Ay, ay. Anything you please—poor creature; don't put yourself in a passion. It'll only make you worse. (Whistles.)

STRANGE GENTLEMAN. This is most extraordinary behaviour. I don't understand it.—What d' ye mean by behaving in this manner? (Rising.)

TOM (aside). He's getting wiolent. I must frighten him with a steady look.—I say, young fellow, do you see this here eye? (Staring at him, and pointing at his own eye.)

STRANGE GENTLEMAN (aside). Do I see his eye!—What can he mean by glaring upon me, with that large round optic!—Ha! a terrible light flashes upon me.—He thought I was 'Swing' this morning. It was an insane delusion.—That eye is an insane eye.—He's a madman!

TOM. Madman! Damme, I think he is a madman with a vengeance

STRANGE GENTLEMAN. He acknowledges it. He is sensible of his misfortune!—Go away—leave the room instantly, and tell them to send somebody else.—Go away!

TOM. Oh, you unhappy lunatic!

STRANGE GENTLEMAN. What a dreadful situation!—I shall be attacked, strangled, smothered, and mangled, by a madman! Where's the bell?

TOM (advancing and brandishing his stick). Leave that 'ere bell alone—leave that 'ere bell alone—and come here!

STRANGE GENTLEMAN. Certainly, Mr. Boots, certainly.—He's going to strangle me. (Going towards table.) Let me pour you out a glass of wine, Mr. Boots—pray do! (Aside.) If he said 'Yes,' I'd throw the decanter at his temple.

TOM. None o' your nonsense.—Sit down there. (Forces him into a chair, L. H.) I'll sit here. (Opposite him, R. H.) Look me full in the face, and I won't hurt you. Move hand, foot, or eye, and you'll never want to move either of 'em again.

STRANGE GENTLEMAN. I'm paralysed with terror.

TOM. Ha! (raising his stick in a threatening attitude.)

STRANGE GENTLEMAN. I'm dumb, Mr. Boots—dumb, sir.

They sit gazing intently on each other; TOM with the

stick raised, as the Act Drop slowly descends.

END OF ACT FIRST

ACT II

SCENE I.—The same as SCENE III, ACT I.

TOM SPARKS discovered in the same attitude watching the STRANGE GENTLEMAN, who has fallen asleep with his head over the back of his Chair.

TOM. He's asleep; poor unhappy wretch! How very mad he looks with his mouth wide open and his eyes shut! (STRANGE GENTLEMAN snores.) Ah! there's a wacant snore; no meaning in it at all. I cou'd ha' told he was out of his senses from the very tone of it. (He snores again.) That's a wery insane snore. I should say he was melancholy mad from the sound of it.

Enter, through C. DOOR, OVERTON, MRS. NOAKES, a Chambermaid, and two Waiters; MRS. NOAKES with a warming-pan, the Maid with a light. STRANGE GENTLEMAN starts up, greatly exhausted.

TOM (starting up in C.). Hallo!—Hallo! keep quiet, young fellow. Keep quiet!

STRANGE GENTLEMAN (L. H.). Out of the way, you savage maniac. Mr. Mayor (crossing to him, R. H.), the person you sent to keep guard over me is a madman, sir. What do you mean by shutting me up with a madman?—what do you mean, sir, I ask?

OVERTON, R. H. C. (aside to STRANGE GENTLEMAN). Bravo! bravo! very good indeed—excellent!

STRANGE GENTLEMAN. Excellent, sir!—It's horrible!—The bare recollection of what I have endured, makes me shudder, down to my very toe-nails.

MRS. NOAKES (R. H.). Poor dear!—Mad people always think other people mad.

STRANGE GENTLEMAN. Poor dear! Ma'am! What the devil do you mean by 'Poor dear?' How dare you have a madman here, ma'am, to assault and terrify the visitors to your establishment?

MRS. NOAKES. Ah! terrify indeed! I'll never have another, to please anybody, you may depend on that, Mr. Overton. (To STRANGE GENTLEMAN.) There, there.—Don't exert yourself, there's a dear.

STRANGE GENTLEMAN (C.). Exert myself!—Damme! it's a mercy I have any life left to exert myself with. It's a special miracle, ma'am, that my existence has not long ago fallen a sacrifice to that sanguinary monster in the leather smalls.

OVERTON, R. C. (aside to STRANGE GENTLEMAN). I never saw any passion more real in my life. Keep it up, it's an admirable joke.

STRANGE GENTLEMAN. Joke!—joke!—Peril a precious life, and call it a joke,—you, a man with a sleek head and a broad-brimmed hat, who ought to know better, calling it a joke.—Are you mad too, sir,—are you mad? (Confronting OVERTON.)

TOM, L. H. (very loud). Keep your hands off. Would you murder the wery mayor, himself, you miserable being?

STRANGE GENTLEMAN. Mr. Mayor, I call upon you to issue your warrant for the instant confinement of that one-eyed Orson in some place of security.

OVERTON (aside, advancing a little). He reminds me that he had better be removed to his bedroom. He is right.—Waiters, carry the gentleman upstairs.—Boots, you will continue to watch him in his bedroom.

STRANGE GENTLEMAN. He continue!—What, am I to be boxed up again with this infuriated animal, and killed off, when he has done playing with me?—I won't go—I won't go—help there, help! (The Waiters cross from R. H. to behind him.)

Enter JOHN JOHNSON hastily, C. DOOR.

JOHN (coming forward L. H.). What on earth is the meaning of this dreadful outcry, which disturbs the whole house?

MRS. NOAKES. Don't be alarmed, sir, I beg.—They're only going to carry an unfortunate gentleman, as is out of his senses, to his bedroom.

STRANGE GENTLEMAN, C. (to JOHN). Constable—constable—do your duty—apprehend these persons—every one of them. Do you hear, officer, do you hear?—(The Waiters seize him by the arms.)—Here—here—you see this. You've seen the assault committed. Take them into custody—off with them.

MRS. NOAKES. Poor creature!—He thinks you are a constable, sir.

JOHN. Unfortunate man! It is the second time to-day that he has been the victim of this strange delusion.

STRANGE GENTLEMAN (breaking from Waiters and going to JOHN L. H.) Unfortunate man!—What, do you think I am mad?

JOHN. Poor fellow! His hopeless condition is pitiable indeed. (Goes up.)

STRANGE GENTLEMAN (returning to C.). They're all mad!—Every one of 'em!

MRS. NOAKES. Come now, come to bed—there's a dear young man, do.

STRANGE GENTLEMAN. Who are you, you shameless old ghost, standing there before company, with a large warming-pan, and asking me to come to bed?—Are you mad?

MRS. NOAKES. Oh! he's getting shocking now. Take him away.—Take him away.

OVERTON. Ah, you had better remove him to his bedroom at once. (The Waiters take him up by the feet and shoulders.)

STRANGE GENTLEMAN. Mind, if I survive this, I'll bring an action of false imprisonment against every one of you. Mark my words—especially against that villainous old mayor.—Mind, I'll do it! (They bear him off, struggling and talking—the others crowding round, and assisting.)

OVERTON (following). How well he does it!

[Exeunt L. H. 1st E.

Enter a Waiter, showing in CHARLES TOMKINS in a travelling coat, C. DOOR.

WAITER (L. H.). This room is disengaged now, sir. There was a gentleman in it, but he has just left it.

CHARLES. Very well, this will do. I may want a bed here to-night, perhaps, waiter.

WAITER. Yes, sir.—Shall I take your card to the bar, sir?

CHARLES. My card!—No, never mind.

WAITER. No name, sir?

CHARLES. No—it doesn't matter.

WAITER (aside, as going out). Another Strange Gentleman!

[Exit Waiter, C. DOOR.

CHARLES. Ah!—(Takes off coat.)—The sun and dust on this long ride have been almost suffocating. I wonder whether Fanny has arrived? If she has—the sooner we start forward on our journey further North the better. Let me see; she would be accompanied by her sister, she said in her note—and they would both be on the look-out for me. Then the best thing I can do is to ask no questions, for the present at all events, and to be on the look-out for them. (Looking towards C. DOOR.) Why here she comes, walking slowly down the long passage, straight towards this room—she can't have seen me yet.—Poor girl, how melancholy she looks! I'll keep in the background for an instant, and give her a joyful surprise (He goes up R. H.)

Enter FANNY, C. DOOR.

FANNY (L. H.). Was ever unhappy girl placed in so dreadful a situation! Friendless, and almost alone, in a strange place—my dear, dear Charles a victim to an attack of mental derangement, and I unable to avow my interest in him, or express my anxious sympathy and solicitude for his sufferings! I cannot bear this dreadful torture of agonising suspense. I must and will see him, let the cost be what it may. (She is going L. H.)

CHARLES (coming forward R. H.). Hist! Fanny!

FANNY (starting and repressing a scream). Ch—Charles—here in this room!

CHARLES. Bodily present, my dear, in this very room. My darling Fanny, let me strain you to my bosom. (Advancing.)

FANNY (shrinking back). N—n—no, dearest Charles, no, not now.—(Aside.)—How flushed he is!

CHARLES. No!—Fanny, this cold reception is a very different one to what I looked forward to meeting with, from you.

FANNY (advancing, and offering the tip of her finger). N—n—no—not cold, Charles; not cold. I do not mean it to be so, indeed.—How is your head, now, dear?

CHARLES. How is my head! After days and weeks of suspense and anxiety, when half our dangerous journey is gained, and I meet you here, to bear you whither you can be made mine for life, you greet me with the tip of your longest finger, and inquire after my head,—Fanny, what can you mean?

FANNY. You—you have startled me rather, Charles.—I thought you had gone to bed.

CHARLES. Gone to bed!—Why I have but this moment arrived.

FANNY (aside). Poor, poor Charles!

CHARLES. Miss Wilson, what am I to—

FANNY. No, no; pray, pray, do not suffer yourself to be excited—

CHARLES. Suffer myself to be excited!—Can I possibly avoid it? can I do aught but wonder at this extraordinary and sudden change in your whole demeanour?—Excited! But five minutes since, I arrived here, brimful of the hope and expectation which had buoyed up my spirits during my long journey. I find you cold, reserved, and embarrassed—everything but what I expected to find you— and then you tell me not to be excited.

FANNY (aside). He is wandering again. The fever is evidently upon him.

CHARLES. This altered manner and ill-disguised confusion all convince me of what you would fain conceal. Miss Wilson, you repent of your former determination, and love another!

FANNY. Poor fellow!

CHARLES. Poor fellow!—What, am I pitied?

FANNY. Oh, Charles, do not give way to this. Consider how much depends upon your being composed.

CHARLES. I see how much depends upon my being composed, ma'am—well, very well.—A husband depends upon it, ma'am. Your new lover is in this house, and if he overhears my reproaches he will become suspicious of the woman who has jilted another, and may jilt him. That's it, madam—a great deal depends, as you say, upon my being composed.—A great deal, ma'am.

FANNY. Alas! these are indeed the ravings of frenzy.

CHARLES. Upon my word, ma'am, you must form a very modest estimate of your own power, if you imagine that disappointment has impaired my senses. Ha, ha, ha!—I am delighted. I am delighted to have escaped you, ma'am. I am glad, ma'am—damn'd glad! (Kicks a chair over.)

FANNY (aside). I must call for assistance. He grows more incoherent and furious every instant.

CHARLES. I leave you ma'am.—I am unwilling to interrupt the tender tête-à-tête with the other gentleman, to which you are, no doubt, anxiously looking forward.—To you I have no more to say. To him I must beg to offer a few rather unexpected congratulations on his approaching marriage.

[Exit CHARLES hastily, C. DOOR.

FANNY. Alas! it is but too true. His senses have entirely left him.

[Exit L. H.

SCENE SECOND AND LAST.—A Gallery in the Inn, leading to the Bedrooms. Four Doors in the Flat, and one at each of the upper Entrances, numbered from 20 to 25, beginning at the R. H. A pair of boots at the door of 23.

 Enter Chambermaid with two lights; and CHARLES TOMKINS,

R. H. 1st E.

MAID. This is your room, sir, No. 21. (Opening the door.)

CHARLES. Very well. Call me at seven in the morning.

MAID. Yes, sir. (Gives him a light, and

[Exit Chambermaid, R. H. 1st E.

CHARLES. And at nine, if I can previously obtain a few words of explanation with this unknown rival, I will just return to the place from whence I came, in the same coach that brought me down here. I wonder who he is and where he sleeps. (Looking round.) I have a lurking suspicion of those boots. (Pointing to No. 23.) They are an ill-looking, underhanded sort of pair, and an undefinable instinct tells me that they have clothed the feet of the rascal I am in search of. Besides myself, the owner of those ugly articles is the only person who has yet come up to bed. I will keep my eyes open for half an hour or so; and my ears too.

[Exit CHARLES into No. 21.

Enter R. H. 1st E. MRS. NOAKES with two lights, followed by MARY and FANNY.

MRS. NOAKES. Take care of the last step, ladies. This way, ma'am, if you please. No. 20 is your room, ladies: nice large double-bedded room, with coals and a rushlight.

FANNY, R. H. (aside to MARY). I must ask which is his room. I cannot rest unless I know he has at length sunk into the slumber he so much needs. (Crosses to MRS. NOAKES, who is L. H.) Which is the room in which the Strange Gentleman sleeps?

MRS. NOAKES. No. 23, ma'am. There's his boots outside the door. Don't be frightened of him, ladies. He's very quiet now, and our Boots is a watching him.

FANNY. Oh, no—we are not afraid of him. (Aside.) Poor Charles!

MRS. NOAKES (going to door No. 20, which is 3rd E. R. H.). This way, if you please; you'll find everything very comfortable, and there's a bell-rope at the head of the bed, if you want anything in the morning. Good night, ladies.

As MARY and FANNY pass MRS. NOAKES, FANNY takes a light.

[Exeunt FANNY and MARY into No. 20.

MRS. NOAKES (tapping at No. 23). Tom—Tom—

Enter TOM from No. 23.

TOM (coming forward, L. H.). Is that you, missis?

MRS. NOAKES (R. H.). Yes.—How's the Strange Gentleman, Tom?

TOM. He was very boisterous half an hour ago, but I punched his head a little, and now he's uncommon comfortable. He's fallen asleep, but his snores is still wery incoherent.

MRS. NOAKES. Mind you take care of him, Tom. They'll take him away in half an hour's time. It's very nearly one o'clock now.

TOM. I'll pay ev'ry possible attention to him. If he offers to call out, I shall whop him again.

[Exit TOM into No. 23.

MRS. NOAKES (looking off R. H.). This way, ma'am, if you please. Up these stairs.

Enter JULIA DOBBS with a light, R. H. 1st E.

JULIA. Which did you say was the room in which I could arrange my dress for travelling?

MRS. NOAKES. No. 22, ma'am; the next room to your nephew's. Poor dear—he's fallen asleep, ma'am, and I dare say you'll be able to take him away very quietly by and by.

JULIA (aside). Not so quietly as you imagine, if he plays his part half as well as Overton reports he does. (To MRS. NOAKES.) Thank you.—For the present, good night.

[Exit JULIA into No. 22.

MRS. NOAKES. Wish you good night, ma'am. There.—Now I think I may go downstairs again, and see if Mr. Overton wants any more negus. Why who's this? (Looking off R. H.) Oh, I forgot—No. 24 an't a-bed yet.—It's him.

Enter JOHN JOHNSON with a light, R. H. 1st E.

MRS. NOAKES. No. 24, sir, if you please.

JOHN. Yes, yes, I know. The same room I slept in last night. (Crossing L. H.)

MRS. NOAKES. Yes, sir.—Wish you good night, sir.

[Exit MRS. NOAKES, R. H. 1st E.

JOHN. Good night, ma'am. The same room I slept in last night, indeed, and the same room I may sleep in to-morrow night, and the next night, and the night after that, and just as many more nights as I can get credit here, unless this remittance arrives. I could raise the money to prosecute my journey without difficulty were I on the spot; but my confounded thoughtless liberality to the post-boys has left me absolutely penniless. Well, we shall see what tomorrow brings forth. (He goes into No. 24, but immediately returns and places his boots outside his room door, leaving it ajar.)

[Exit JOHN into No. 24.

CHARLES peeping from No. 21, and putting out his boots.

CHARLES. There's another pair of boots. Now I wonder which of these two fellows is the man. I can't help thinking it's No. 23.—Hallo! (He goes in and closes his door.)

The door of No. 20 opens; FANNY comes out with a light in a night shade. No. 23 opens. She retires into No. 20.

Enter TOM SPARKS, with a stable lantern from No. 23.

TOM (closing the door gently). Fast asleep still. I may as vell go my rounds, and glean for the deputy. (Pulls out a piece of chalk from his pocket, and takes up boots from No. 23.) Twenty-three. It's difficult to tell what a fellow is ven he han't got his senses, but I think this here twenty-three's a timorous faint-hearted genus. (Examines the boots.) You want new soleing, No. 23. (Goes to No. 24, takes up boots and looks at them.) Hallo! here's a bust: and there's been a piece put on in the corner.—I must let my missis know. The bill's always doubtful ven there's any mending. (Goes to No. 21, takes up boots.) French calf Vellingtons.—All's right here. These here French calves always come it strong—light vines, and all that 'ere. (Looking round.) Werry happy to see there an't no high-lows—they never drinks nothing but gin-and-vater. Them and the cloth boots is the vurst customers an inn has.—The cloth boots is always obstemious, only drinks sherry vine and vater, and never eats no suppers. (He chalks the No. of the room on each pair of boots as he takes them up.) Lucky for you, my French calves, that you an't done with the patent polish, or you'd ha' been witrioled in no time. I don't like to put oil o' witriol on a well-made pair of boots; ben ven they're rubbed vith that 'ere polish, it must be done, or the profession's ruined.

[Exit TOM with boots, R. H. 1st E.

Enter FANNY from No. 20, with light as before.

FANNY. I tremble at the idea of going into his room, but surely at a moment like this, when he is left to be attended by rude and uninterested strangers, the strict rules of propriety which regulate our ordinary proceedings may be dispensed with. I will but satisfy myself that he sleeps, and has those comforts which his melancholy situation demands, and return immediately. (Goes to No. 23, and knocks.)

CHARLES TOMKINS peeping from No. 21.

CHARLES. I'll swear I heard a knock.—A woman! Fanny Wilson—and at that door at this hour of the night!

FANNY comes forward.

Why what an ass I must have been ever to have loved that girl. It is No 23, though.—I'll throttle him presently. The next room-door open—I'll watch there. (He crosses to No. 24, and goes in.)

FANNY returns to No. 23, and knocks—the door opens and the STRANGE GENTLEMAN appears, night-cap on his head and a light in his hand.—FANNY screams and runs back into No. 20.

STRANGE GENTLEMAN (coming forward). Well, of all the wonderful and extraordinary houses that ever did exist, this particular tenement is the most extraordinary. I've got rid of the madman at last—and it's almost time for that vile old mayor to remove me. But where?—I'm lost, bewildered, confused, and actually begin to think I am mad. Half these things I've seen to-day must be visions of fancy—they never could have really happened. No, no, I'm clearly mad!—I've not the least doubt of it now. I've caught it from that horrid Boots. He has inoculated the whole establishment. We're all mad together.—(Looking off R. H.) Lights coming upstairs!—Some more lunatics.

[Exit STRANGE GENTLEMAN in No. 23.

Enter R. H. 1st E. OVERTON with a cloak, MRS. NOAKES, TOM SPARKS with lantern, and three Waiters with lights. The Waiters range up R. H. side. TOM is in R. H. corner and MRS. NOAKES next to him.

OVERTON. Remain there till I call for your assistance. (Goes up to No. 23 and knocks.)

Enter STRANGE GENTLEMAN from No. 23.

Now, the chaise is ready.—Muffle yourself up in this cloak. (Puts it on the STRANGE GENTLEMAN.—They come forward.)

STRANGE GENTLEMAN (L. H.). Yes.

OVERTON (C.). Make a little noise when we take you away, you know.

STRANGE GENTLEMAN. Yes—yes.—I say, what a queer room this is of mine. Somebody has been tapping at the wall for the last half hour, like a whole forest of woodpeckers.

OVERTON. Don't you know who that was?

STRANGE GENTLEMAN. No.

OVERTON. The other party.

STRANGE GENTLEMAN (alarmed). The other party!

OVERTON. To be sure. The other party is going with you.

STRANGE GENTLEMAN. Going with me!—In the same chaise!

OVERTON. Of course.—Hush! (Goes to No. 22. Knocks.)

Enter JULIA DOBBS from No. 22, wrapped up in a large cloak.

Look here! (Bringing her forward. JULIA is next to MRS. NOAKES.)

STRANGE GENTLEMAN (starting into L. H. CORNER). I won't go—I won't go. This is a plot—a conspiracy. I won't go, I tell you. I shall be assassinated.—I shall be murdered!

FANNY and MARY appear at No. 20, JOHNSON and TOMKINS at 24.

JOHN (at the door). I told you he was mad.

CHARLES (at the door). I see—I see—poor fellow!

JULIA (crossing to STRANGE GENTLEMAN and taking his arm). Come, dear, come.

MRS. NOAKES. Yes, do go, there's a good soul. Go with your affectionate aunt.

STRANGE GENTLEMAN (breaking from her). My affectionate aunt!

JULIA returns to her former position.

TOM. He don't deserve no affection. I niver see such an unfectionate fellow to his relations.

STRANGE GENTLEMAN (L. H.). Take that wretch away, and smother him between two feather beds. Take him away, and make a sandwich of him directly.

JULIA (to OVERTON, who is in C.). What voice was that?—It was not Lord Peter's. (Throwing off her cloak.)

OVERTON. Nonsense—nonsense.—Look at him. (Pulls cloak off STRANGE GENTLEMAN.)

STRANGE GENTLEMAN (turning round). A woman!

JULIA. A stranger!

OVERTON. A stranger! What, an't he your husband that is to—your mad nephew, I mean?

JULIA. No!

ALL. No!

STRANGE GENTLEMAN. No!—no, I'll be damned if I am. I an't anybody's nephew.—My aunt's dead, and I never had an uncle.

MRS. NOAKES. And an't he mad, ma'am?

JULIA. No.

STRANGE GENTLEMAN. Oh, I'm not mad.—I was mistaken just now.

OVERTON. And isn't he going away with you?

JULIA. No.

MARY (coming forward R. H., next to MRS. NOAKES). And isn't his name Tomkins?

STRANGE GENTLEMAN (very loud.) No.

(All these questions and answers should be very rapid. JOHNSON and TOMKINS advance to the ladies, and they all retire up.)

MRS. NOAKES. What is his name? (Producing a letter.) It an't Mr. Walker Trott, is it? (She advances a little towards him.)

STRANGE GENTLEMAN. Something so remarkably like it, ma'am, that, with your permission, I'll open that epistle. (Taking letter.)

All go up, but JULIA and STRANGE GENTLEMAN.

(Opening letter.) Tinkles's hand. (Reads.) 'The challenge was a ruse. By this time I shall have been united at Gretna Green to the charming Emily Brown.'—Then, through a horror of duels, I have lost a wife!

JULIA (R. H. with her handkerchief to her eyes). And through Lord Peter's negligence, I have lost a husband!

STRANGE GENTLEMAN. Eh! (Regards her for a moment, then beckons OVERTON, who comes forward, L. H.) I say, didn't you say something about three thousand a year this morning?

OVERTON. I did.

STRANGE GENTLEMAN. You alluded to that party? (Nodding towards JULIA.)

OVERTON. I did.

STRANGE GENTLEMAN. Hem! (Puts OVERTON back). Permit me, ma'am (going to her), to sympathise most respectfully with your deep distress.

JULIA. Oh, sir! your kindness penetrates to my very heart.

STRANGE GENTLEMAN (aside). Penetrates to her heart!—It's taking the right direction.—If I understand your sorrowing murmur, ma'am, you contemplated taking a destined husband away with you, in the chaise at the door?

JULIA. Oh! sir,—spare my feelings—I did.—The horses were ordered and paid for; and everything was ready. (Weeps.)

STRANGE GENTLEMAN (aside). She weeps.—Expensive thing, posting, ma'am.

JULIA. Very, sir.

STRANGE GENTLEMAN. Eighteen-pence a mile, ma'am, not including the boys.

JULIA. Yes, sir.

STRANGE GENTLEMAN. You've lost a husband, ma'am—I have lost a wife.—Marriages are made above—I'm quite certain ours is booked.—Pity to have all this expense for nothing—let's go together.

JULIA (drying her eyes).The suddenness of this proposal, sir—

STRANGE GENTLEMAN. Requires a sudden answer, ma'am.—You don't say no—you mean yes. Permit me to—(kisses her).—All right! Old one (to OVERTON, who comes down L. H.), I've done it.— Mrs. Noakes (she comes down R. H.), don't countermand the chaise.—We're off directly.

CHARLES (who with FANNY comes down L. H. C.). So are we.

JOHN (who with MARY come down R. H. C.). So are we, thanks to a negotiated loan, and an explanation as hasty as the quarrel that gave rise to it.

STRANGE GENTLEMAN. Three post-chaises and four, on to Gretna, directly.

[Exeunt Waiters, R. H. 1st E.

I say—we'll stop here as we come back?

JOHN and CHARLES. Certainly.

STRANGE GENTLEMAN. But before I go, as I fear I have given a great deal of trouble here to-night— permit me to inquire whether you will view my mistakes and perils with an indulgent eye, and consent to receive 'The Strange Gentleman' again to-morrow.

CURTAIN.

Charles Dickens - A Short Biography

Charles Dickens (1812-1870) is regarded by many readers and literary critics to be THE major English novelist of the Victorian Age. He is remembered today as the author of a series of weighty novels which have been translated into many languages and promoted to the rank of World Classics. The latter include, but are not limited to, *The Adventures of Oliver Twist*, *A Tale of Two Cities*, *David Copperfield*, *A Christmas Carol*, *Hard Times*, *Great Expectations* and *The Old Curiosity Shop*.

Birth and Childhood's Hardships

By and large, Charles Dickens's life story is one of somebody who is born and raised in dire straits to become one of the greatest men who have marked human history and thought. It is a perfect example of how the plight of the deprived and the destitute could transform into a precious incentive that pushes them to challenge their circumstances and to unexpectedly excel and shine.

Charles Dickens was born in Portsmouth on February 7th, 1812. His father John Dickens worked as a simple accounting clerk at the Naval Pay Office and the family's pecuniary situation was almost always uneven. When Charles was only two years, the family had to move to London, then later to Chatham. For financial reasons, Charles did not have adequate education. He rather had to leave school at a very young age to work at a polishing and blacking factory. To add insult to injury, Charles's father was imprisoned in 1824 after failing to pay a 40-pound debt.

Charles's experience at the factory played a tremendous role in building the novelist's personality and in deepening his concerns about working children and about the working class in general. Dickens's precocious maturity and the serious responsibilities that he had as a little child left a clear impression on many of his young characters, such as Oliver Twist, David Copperfield and Pip in *Great Expectations*. The hardships that Charles Dickens personally went through made him much interested in defending the poor, in fighting social injustice through exposing its blatant manifestations and in accentuating the importance of having decent work conditions.

Between 1824 and 1827, Dickens's father, who eventually managed to pay his debts, offered Charles the opportunity to attend a private school in North London, the Wellington House Academy. The experience surely enriched the young man's knowledge of the rules of writing and rhetoric and whetted his appetite for 18th-century novels and for the picaresque novels that adorned his father's library. However, during this period, Charles still had to experience another disappointment when his mother refused to spare him the strenuous job at the blacking factory even after the relative improvement of the family's financial situation. The mother's decision had a great psychological impact on young Charles and even influenced his vision of gender roles as he thought that the mother should not be the decision-maker in the family.

Early Publications

Young Charles Dickens occupied numerous jobs and worked hard to learn shorthand. This long and diversified professional experience had a patent impact on his different writings. Indeed, after the blacking factory experience, Dickens first worked as a clerk for attorneys, which allowed him to learn about the legal system and its principles, to become a free-lance reporter for Doctor's Commons Courts in 1829. Later, he even wrote reports for the House of Commons before starting to work for newspapers, magazines and journals.

It was in 1833 that Dickens started writing short stories for a number of literary magazines and journals such as *The Monthly Magazine.* A collection of these texts was later pseudonymously published under the title *Sketches by Boz.* Thanks to Dickens's humor and exceptional writing style, the latter publication was relatively successful, but not as successful as *The Pickwick Papers* whose serial publication sold thousands of copies and raised Dickens to considerable fame. In 1836, he started writing short texts to be published with the humorous illustrations of the famous artist Robert Seymour. These first successes encouraged Dickens to carry on publishing other stories in the form of series. Dickens's next creation was *Oliver Twist* which was published between 1837 and 1839.

It is noteworthy that most of Dickens's novels were published in the form of monthly and weekly chapters which, according to critics and biographers, allowed him to evaluate and adjust his characterizations and plots to meet the expectations of his readership. It was also during this period that Dickens started his long career as a literary magazine editor.

Loves and Marriage

Charles Dickens got married on April 2nd, 1836 to Catherine Thomson Hogarth after one year of engagement. They settled at the famous Furnival's Inn in Holborn, London, before they moved to their home in Bloomsbury. The house was transformed into the Charles Dickens Museum in 1925. Charles and Catherine, who lived there with the first three of their ten children, were joined by Charles's brother Frederick and Catherine's sister Mary. The latter was reported to have had a very special place in Charles's heart. After dying in his own arms in 1837 following a sudden illness, she became a source of inspiration for some of his female characters. After three years of marriage, Dickens's success and rising income made him leave the house for larger and more luxurious estates.

Catherine Hogarth was not Dickens's only love, however. Indeed, biographers report that Dickens's relation with his wife was sandwiched by two other romantic affairs. First, there was Maria Beadnell, a banker's daughter, with whom Dickens fell in love when he was only eighteen years old. The relationship ended three years later when Maria's parents apparently intervened. The other love story that Dickens went through started in 1857 and pushed him to divorce Catherine the following year. It was when Dickens was having a group of young actresses for the staging of his play *The Frozen Deep* that he fell in love with the actress Ellen Ternan who was 27 years younger than him.

Major Achievements

Charles's first success with *The Pickwick Papers* and *Oliver Twist* only pushed him to devote more time and energy to his writing and editorial activities. After publishing *Nicholas Nickleby* between 1838 and 1839, he started a new project in 1840 that he entitled *Master Humphrey's Clock*. The latter is a collection of stories that share the same frame and have recurring characters. It was among this collection that the two major works *The Old Curiosity Shop* and *Barnaby Rudge* were serially published.

After visiting the United States of America in 1842, Dickens developed a rather negative view of the New World which was mainly depicted in his travelogue *American Notes for General Circulation* and also in his picaresque novel *Martin Chuzzlewit*. The latter included very harsh satire of the republic and strongly denounced its institution of slavery. However, the fury that Dickens caused among some American circles was soon quietened with the publication of *A Christmas Carol* in 1843. The book, which is considered by many as the novelist's finest opus, was celebrated both in England and America.

Two other Christmas books followed respectively in 1834 and 1845. They are *The Chimes* and *The Cricket on the Hearth*. During this period, Dickens also published a new travelogue that he entitled *Pictures from Italy* following his stay in the Mediterranean country. Another Christmas story entitled *The Haunted Man* was published in 1848, which was preceded by *Dombey and Son* (1847) and *The Battle of Life* (1847) and followed by David Copperfield (1849-1850), *Bleak House* (1852-1853) and *Hard Times* (1854).

It was in 1853 that Dickens started organizing public performances in which he presented his literary works. By this time, he also started to collaborate with Wilkie Collins on a number of short stories and plays. *Little Dorrit* started as a monthly serial in 1855 to be finished in 1857. Later, two of Dickens's most valuable works were published: *A Tale of Two Cities* (1859) and *Great Expectations* (1861). They were both published in the weekly periodical, *All the Year Round*, which he founded and edited himself.

Apart from his writings, Dickens's main profitable activity was the public reading of his novels. Along with the money he earned thanks to his successful publications, public readings allowed Dickens to buy his dream house (Gad's Hill Place, Kent), to offer financial help to his parents and brothers and to engage in charitable activities.

Twilight and Death

During the 1860s, Dickens carried on organizing more reading tours. In addition to the many events he had in England, he visited France, the United States, Scotland and Ireland on many an occasion. In 1864, he started his last complete novel, *Our Mutual Friend*. However, by 1865, his health started to waver. This was mainly because of the physical and intellectual exhaustion to which he subjected himself. Furthermore, Dickens was psychologically traumatized in 1865 following a train crash. He was with his beloved Ellen Ternan on their way back from Paris when their train derailed to cause a big number of casualties. Although Dickens was able to collect his courage and managed to help the wounded and comfort them, the picture of the disaster affected him greatly and could never be erased from his mind.

For health reasons, Dickens cancelled many of his programmed readings between 1868 and 1870. On April 22nd, 1869, he had a stroke. The latter was followed by a second stroke on June 8th, 1870, while he was working on his novel *The Mystery of Edwin Drood* which would remain unfinished. The next day, he passed away. Charles Dickens today rests in The Poets' Corner of Westminster Abbey.

www.ingramcontent.com/pod-product-compliance
Lightning Source LLC
Chambersburg PA
CBHW061010405042 6
4244 8CB000 11B/2612